ALL ABOUT ADOPTION

how to deal with the questions of your past

all about ADOPTION

how to deal with the questions of your past

by Anne Lanchon
illustrated by Monike Czarnecki
edited by Tucker Shaw

sunscreen

Book series design by Higashi Glaser Design
Production Manager: Jonathan Lopes

Library of Congress Cataloging-in-Publication Data:
Lanchon, Anne.
[Adoption, des ados en parlent. English]
Adoption : how to deal with the questions of your past / Anne Lanchon ; illustrated by
Monike Czarnecki ; edited by Tucker Shaw.
p. cm. — (Sunscreen)
Original French title: L'Adoption, des ados en parlent.
ISBN 0-8109-9227-2
1. Adoption. I. Shaw, Tucker. II. Title. III. Series.

HV875.L226 2006
649'.145—dc22
2005011778

Translated by JMS Books, LLC

Published in 2006 by Amulet Books
an imprint of Harry N. Abrams, Incorporated
115 West 18th Street
New York, NY 10011
www.abramsbooks.com

Printed and bound in China
10 9 8 7 6 5 4 3 2 1

Abrams is a subsidiary of

LA MARTINIÈRE

contents

phase 2: MY FAMILY

phase 3: WHERE DID I COME FROM?

ADOPTED OR NOT, YOU'RE A TEEN JUST LIKE EVERYONE ELSE

Let's face it: Being a teenager is jam-packed with constant challenges. No matter how strong, confident, unique, and intelligent you are, it can be a bumpy ride. And sometimes there's a lot to deal with. There's school. Friendships. Love. Peer pressure. Body issues. Driving. Physical changes. College deadlines. Sex. No wonder being a teen can be such a crazy time.

And, oh yeah, let's not forget family issues. There's that, too. Curfews. Fights. Expectations. Disappointments. Sometimes it's a real love-hate relationship with your family.

Only, since you're adopted and your parents aren't your birth parents, your family issues are a little different. OK, a lot different. It's not like your family relationships are any less strong or important, but it adds a whole extra layer to who you are. And, just like everything else you have to deal with, it's not always easy to cope.

Don't worry. Your situation might be unique, but when all is said and done, you're no weirder than anyone else. You're adopted, your friends aren't, so what?

This book can't answer all the questions you have about your adoption. But there are issues that most adopted kids think about every now and then, and this book has ideas to help you work through them. It will help you figure out what your questions are, and where to look for answers.

Abandonment

WHO

What other people think

I prefer to hide the fact that I'm adopted

I don't look like anyone in my family

Don't blame everything on being adopted

AM I?

Who will I look like when I grow up?

i'm just like

everyone
else

Let's start with Alex. He's fifteen, adopted, and not really interested in talking about it. It's been nine years since he left Russia and he feels 100 percent American. Just like other teens, his top priorities are friends, school, tennis, and video games. He almost never thinks about Russia, or wonders about his birth parents. He's even lost his accent.

Like Alex, many young people who have been adopted have absolutely no interest in looking back at their birth history. At least, that's the way it seems. They see their adoptive parents as their real parents and they feel that their adoption has had no effect on their character or their relationships with other people. Or let's take Nick. He's thirteen, adopted, and, he explains, "I'm just a regular guy like all the others. Even though, when I think about it, my history is definitely different."

Sound strange? Well, there are a couple reasons why Alex and Nick feel this way. For one thing, they're teenagers, just like you. That means there's just so much going on (puberty, peer pressure, school, dating . . . you name it) that your early childhood may be the last thing you have time or interest in thinking about. You've got plenty to keep you busy and plenty to obsess about as it is, thanks.

Plus, it's not like being adopted is some crazy thing. Sure, it's a special situation, but there are over 150,000 kids adopted in the United States every year. It's not that unusual.

And no, you're not that weird.

In fact, every family has their own issues. Look around. Some families have two parents, two kids, and a dog. But many families have one

parent. Or two parents of the same sex. Or two parents of different religions or races. Some families have two sets of triplets and a parrot. Every family is different. And people don't consider adoption strange at all. They don't give it a second thought.

This is a good thing. Because, believe it or not, many years ago, adoption was a huge secret for many. Parents would secretly adopt a child because they were ashamed that they weren't able to have children for medical reasons. And then they wouldn't tell the child because they feared he or she would feel badly about being adopted. Can you imagine?

Good thing these attitudes have changed. Adoption is accepted for what it truly is—a good thing! It's an amazing gift to the parents and a gift to the child. And it is celebrated.

So, for all these reasons, Nick, Alex, and many other adopted teens don't obsess about being adopted at all.

i don't like talking about being
adopted

Some adopted teenagers, even though they're totally cool with having been adopted and love their adoptive parents, don't like to talk about it. Maybe they don't want to emphasize their differences. Maybe, like most teenagers, they're focused on fitting in and being a normal teen, rather than focused on what makes them different.

It makes sense, if you think about it. No one really likes to be an outsider, especially teenagers. Look around your school: Everyone's wearing the same clothes, carrying the same backpacks, using the same slang. Trying to fit in is a normal phase to go through and it's an important part of growing up. So it makes sense that some adopted teenagers don't want to broadcast the fact that they're different.

Some adopted teenagers prefer to keep their history in a box somewhere, and try not to think about it. Some adopted teenagers who were born in other parts of the world may have no desire to ever visit their countries of origin or to learn their native languages. These teenagers aren't embarrassed or ashamed of their beginnings, they're just thinking about the present. After all, America is where they live now, so they might as well focus on the current situation.

i prefer to hide the fact that i'm
adopted

Some young people who are less comfortable about being adopted prefer to hide it from the people around them whenever possible. They are afraid of being judged or identified as different. (Kind of like every teenager on the planet!)

One adopted teen, Tatiana, remembers, "I never talked about it with my friends. I'm sure they knew, but they acted as if they didn't. I even told them that my brothers and sisters were adopted and that I

was the only biological daughter in the family. But one day my teacher, thinking he was doing the right thing, asked me in front of the whole class if I would talk to them about being adopted. I wanted to die of embarrassment because of all the little white lies I told."

Not everyone's like Tatiana. But many adopted kids just want to keep their stories to themselves. After all, it's a pretty personal thing. It can be complicated and confusing enough for you, let alone for anyone else.

You may not want to share your story, and that's totally under-standable. After all, non-adopted kids don't have to rehash their early years all the time or explain their situations. So why should you? But you shouldn't be afraid or embarrassed to do so, either. You have nothing to hide because you were adopted.

Thomas, like many adopted kids, gets annoyed when his mother feels like she has to tell everyone about how he was adopted from Southeast Asia. "She tells everyone," complains Thomas. "She tells the checkout person at the store, all of her friends, everyone at the gym. I hate it because it's like everyone's talking *about* me, instead of talking *to* me."

The thing is, Thomas's mother is just really proud of him, and proud to be a part of his life. It may be annoying sometimes, but she just wants to share. If your family's the same way, it can't hurt to let them know how you feel. So speak up!

what other people think

Even though adoption is totally common these days, some people still don't know how to deal with it. They say things like, "Oh . . . I didn't know." Or "I'm sorry."

Sorry for what? Anne, an adopted teenager, says, "It might be different, but it's not something to be sorry about! I've always been very happy with it and I wouldn't change my parents for the world!"

People say things like "I'm sorry" because they only see the potential negative side of your adoption (which is the absence of your birth parents). They totally ignore what it's really about, which is the loving presence of your adoptive parents. They figure that if you're adopted, you must be an orphan, and that your life must have been like Oliver Twist's, left to fend for himself, beg for food, and fight off evil grownups. Imagine if you had to walk around in knickers saying "Please, sir, may I have some more?"

So, it falls on you to reassure them that you're OK, that you have parents, that your life isn't all that different from theirs. Sometimes all this reassuring of everyone else can get really exhausting. It's enough for you to deal with, why do you have to coach everyone else through it, too?

You've heard all the questions. "How old were you when you were adopted?" "Do you know who your birth parents are?" "Do you want to meet them?" You know that they're just curious, and they're not trying to be annoying, but the fact is you kind of get sick of answering these questions all the time. It puts you in the hot seat, and places you in a

position where you have to explain yourself. Talk about a squirm-worthy situation. If other teens don't have to do this, then you feel you shouldn't either!

Besides, you might not even have all the answers. Alice, an adopted teen who doesn't know exactly where her birth parents came from, says, "My friends discuss my background for hours. Some think I come from North Africa, others think I come from Latin America. It's really strange hearing them talk about it, trying to figure out the answers when even I don't know them."

Remember, even though sometimes it feels like everyone has their noses all up in your business, sometimes you just have to let them talk. Remember, you're not the only one with a special backstory. Yours just seems to be the most popular one to talk about! It's OK to let it fly right on past you—or if you want, dig right in and talk about it all day long. It's up to you.

i don't like the way i look

Most of the time, adopted kids don't look like their parents. This, of course, makes total sense. Sometimes your nose is a little different, or you have dark hair while they have light hair, or you have a different ethnic background altogether. It makes it hard to "hide" the fact that you were adopted, and also acts as a frequent reminder about the differences between you and your family.

It's normal to feel insecure about your looks, especially as a teenager. It seems like everyone wants a different body, or different hair, or less acne. Rest assured, this is totally normal and everyone feels this way, even the most popular kids you know.

But your struggle with the way you look does have a whole extra layer to it. You don't have parents who look like you to use as role models. And you wonder if they really understand what you're going through. Sure, they love you, but they don't look like you. How can they have any clue? "I think I would have been able to accept being adopted more easily if I had been white," admits Thomas, who was born in India. "Sometimes I wonder what life would be like if I looked more like my parents."

people make racist comments
about me

Sometimes the tough stuff you have to go through isn't just about the fact that you're adopted. Sometimes, for some adoptees, it's just straight-up racism. You may find yourself dealing with racial comments. You might even feel threatened because of your race.

And when you let your parents know about the difficulties you're going through, no matter how much they try to understand, no matter how hard they work to make your life smoother, if they're not from the same racial background as you are, you still feel like they don't totally get it. You may even feel like they can't really help.

This is totally understandable. Again, it's that extra layer you have to deal with. But if this kind of thing is happening to you, you have to let your adoptive parents in on it. No one has the right to harass you for your skin color or ethnic makeup, and there are ways that your parents can help. For one thing, they're an amazing source of confidence and strength, and even though they don't understand exactly what it's like to be in your shoes, they love you as strongly as any other parent. And this love is where you'll get the strength you need to handle the hard times.

i don't look like anyone in
my family

As a teenager, it's totally normal to worry about the way you look. Everyone goes through it. But with you, surprise, surprise—there's a little extra to deal with.

So you don't look exactly like your family. It doesn't sound like that big of a deal, right? Well . . . sort of.

When a baby is born into a family, everyone falls all over themselves to exclaim how beautiful the infant is (even if it isn't, and let's face it, some newborns can look pretty scrunchie-faced, but that's another story . . .). People can't wait to start looking for family resemblances: "He has his father's green eyes, his grandmother's pretty smile. . . ."

This slightly irritating attitude is a way of welcoming the newborn and telling him that he belongs in his family. And it doesn't let up. People are constantly saying things like "He's a real chip off the old block!" (gag) and "She's the spitting image of her mom!" (double gag). But even though it can be annoying to hear such things, these kinds of comments reassure non-adopted children that they're part of a biological family tree.

With adopted children, it's not quite the same. For the most part, no one will ever say that you look like your mom or your grandfather. And no matter how much you know that your parents love you, it can be painful not to look like anyone in your family. It can make you feel like you don't quite belong.

Some adopted kids even go so far as to try and find characteristics that are similar to their parents. Even though Alex was born in Russia, and his adoptive family is in Ohio, he still identifies completely with his adoptive father. "It's natural that I'm tall, because my dad is 6' 3"!" he told his mom.

who will i look like when i
grow up?

All teenagers, adopted or not, have to go through all the drama and chaos of puberty. You're being bombarded with hormones, and your body is changing wildly. You can't keep up with the number of new places you're sprouting hair. Some of you are growing breasts, some of you are getting deeper voices. And none of it is easy to deal with. But guess what, you have to deal.

When you're not adopted, at least you know, sort of, what you might look like later on in life. Parents serve as a good reference point. (By the way, this can be comforting, or totally scary!)

But when you are adopted, it's all a total mystery. You have no idea how tall you'll be, how big your feet will be, whether you'll lose your hair, or how big your boobs will get. "I was very anxious because I didn't know who I was going to look like later," Alice remembers. "I didn't know whether my birth mother was tall or short, whether she'd had bad acne, or how old she was when she started her periods."

Not knowing these things can worry you a bit but it also causes your parents a fair amount of concern. They can't answer all your questions, especially those about your background. However, their experience is still really useful. They've been around the block once or twice, whether you share the same genes or not.

abandonment

One of the hardest things to make sense of when you're adopted is understanding why your life started this way. You probably have gone through complicated feelings of being "abandoned" as a baby or young child, and you wondered why. Maybe it's because your parents died, or maybe your parents, for economic or emotional issues, didn't feel that they could be good parents. Maybe you came from a region of the world that's going through crisis. There are all kinds of reasons why feelings of abandonment might be there.

Strong feelings might be inside you, even if you don't use the word "abandonment" to describe them. You say, "My mother gave me away," or "My father didn't want me." These feelings of abandonment can run deep, and almost all adopted children feel it at one time or another. It's totally normal.

Everyone tells you that it's better this way, or that you're better off having been adopted. Your adoption was a blessing and it was for your own good. Blah, blah, blah.

But sometimes it feels strange. Isn't a child supposed to grow up with his or her mother, no matter what? These feelings cause pain, and no explanation can get rid of it. Felicia, a fourteen-year-old, explains, "I just can't accept the idea that my mother couldn't deal with me." Even though Felicia has a wonderful relationship with her adoptive family, she says, "Sometimes I feel like I was just thrown away."

the usual questions

So what does it mean to feel abandoned? You might start thinking, "My parents didn't keep me because I was not worthy of staying with them." Or "I'm worthless and my mom was right to do what she did!"

On the other hand, you might think, "If I'm so great, then my mother must have been a really bad person to give me away. Am I going to grow up to be just like her?"

These may or may not be the same thoughts that you're having, but it's common for adopted teenagers to think this way. These questions can contribute to feelings of low self-esteem.

And low self-esteem can totally affect your behavior. At school, for example, sometimes troubled teenagers will blow off work, fail on purpose, pick fights, cause trouble, or even worse. It's almost like they want to live up to the "worthlessness" that they feel.

Other troubled teenagers sometimes sink into a deep depression, pulling away from others, not believing that they're worthy of the friendships and relationships other teens enjoy. They feel terribly alone.

These feelings can also mess with their ideas about their adoptive parents. There's a common feeling that adopted kids have: If they were abandoned already, why would their new parents want them forever? It sounds harsh, but sometimes adopted kids feel this way.

If you're going through these feelings, if they're floating around your head and keeping you up all night, it's important to talk about them. It's true that your parents can't necessarily solve your problems, but they can definitely help you understand them, and help you find the confidence you need to deal with them better.

One thing that many psychologists try to help adopted kids remember is that although birth parents gave them up for adoption, they did it for the right reasons. In other words, it's very likely that your mother entrusted you to your adoptive parents because she loved you so much.

Another thing to keep in mind is that you are a very different person now than who you were as a baby. When the adoption took place, it wasn't because of a judgment about *you.* It was because of circumstances that had nothing to do with you or who you are.

being adopted
later in life

The thing about adoption is that everyone's story is different. While some adopted kids found their families when they were still babies, others were adopted later, when they were three, four, or even ten or twelve years old.

The first few years of a child's life are very important for his or her emotional development. Children born to loving parents, or children who find loving parents very early on, are surrounded with love, encouragement, and kindness during these years.

But some adopted kids have different stories. They were cared for with many other kids in orphanages, or perhaps they came from abusive homes where they weren't treated as they should have been. Kids with these stories often struggle even more with feelings of acceptance and abandonment.

It's important for all adopted kids to reach out and be as honest as they can about their feelings so they can deal with them. It's critical to find people to talk to.

i'm afraid of being abandoned by
my friends

Everyone's got a different way of dealing with their friendships. Some super-social people have a whole huge posse of friends, welcoming new ones all the time. Some people stick to two or three good friends for life. Some people are in the middle. Your friendship style depends on your personality, and has very little to do with whether you were adopted or not.

But sometimes, for adopted kids, that "extra layer" of being adopted can add an extra layer to your friendships, too. For some adopted kids, those lingering issues of abandonment play into their friendships at school and around town.

One example is Katie, who hates being alone. She calls her friends every time she has to make a decision, whether it's what to wear or what to bring for lunch. She showers them with gifts and goes out of her way to be nice, then gets a little disappointed when they don't do the same for her. She can't go out with a boy without obsessing about when she'll be dumped. This, of course, kind of ruins the date.

For other adopted kids, the fear of being abandoned sometimes has completely the opposite effect. Because they're afraid of being disappointed or rejected at some point, they refuse to get themselves into friendships in the first place, limiting themselves to the fewest number of friends possible. They keep their friends at a distance, trying to protect themselves from being dissed sometime in the future.

Confused yet? Here's the bottom line: Friendships are about respect, kindness, and honesty—whether you're adopted or not. It's important to have friendships because you get support and feedback, not to mention someone to bug out with and crack jokes with when you need to. Friends matter, big time, and whatever your circumstance (adopted or not) it's worth it to pursue them.

don't blame everything on being
adopted

So you've learned a thing or two about the extra layer that being adopted adds to your life, and how this can cause some real problems sometimes. But you have to be careful not to blame all of your problems on being adopted. Just look around—your non-adopted friends are going through their own dramas, their own problems, and they look a lot like yours—annoying parents, insecurity, confusion, and frustration.

Adopted and non-adopted kids both have it rough during the teenage years. Let's be honest, sometimes being a teenager can seriously be a lot to deal with. (Ask anyone you want.) You're trying to find the way from being a child to being an adult, and as excited and impatient as you are about it, it's not exactly an easy road to follow.

But adopted kids sometimes find it easy to blame all of their feelings, all of their struggles, on their adoption. It's an easy thing to do. But keep in mind that it's not the source of all your frustrations. You can also blame the simple fact that you're a teenager.

Sometimes the world makes it easy for you to blame adoption. You've heard people try to explain your behavior using "He was

adopted" or "She was adopted" as an answer, as if this is justification for everything. Some annoying people assume that it's inevitable that you'll have a harder life because of your adoption. But you know better. You've seen non-adopted kids act *way* crazier than you.

The best way to put your mind at ease about everything is to take a good, hard look at what goes on in your friends' lives. That's all it takes to realize that no one's life is perfect. Everyone has their own set of problems and frustrations. It's normal for teens to struggle, adopted or not.

Your parents and
your background

Parents who don't
do enough

MY

The legacy of adoption

Parents who try to make
everything all right

FAMILY

The extended family

parents like any
others

Let's face it, adopted or not, your parents aren't perfect. Sure, you love them, and sure, you admire them, but sometimes they're too strict, too uncool, or just too annoying. Your allowance is pretty meager, you hate your curfew, and you wish they'd get off your back about your grades.

Just like non-adopted children, your relationship with your parents can be frustrating. One moment you'll be getting along great, then all of a sudden they'll upset you. One moment you feel like they totally trust you, then you turn around and they're all over you.

It's the same in every family. Parents are people, and while they usually do their best to give you confidence, good values, and strong character traits, it's eventually up to you to accept or refuse their direction. Adopted or not, you may or may not share your parents' ideals.

Didn't I ask you to tidy your room?

It is tidy...

Even non-adopted children feel like aliens at the dinner table sometimes, and adopted children feel like a mirror image of their parents every now and then.

"I adore my parents, but they are total opposites from me," says Alice. "I am more impulsive; they are set in their ways. I believe in God, but they are atheists. But I still love them and I'm totally comfortable having been adopted by them. Besides, how many non-adopted kids do you know who are complete opposites from their parents? A lot!"

your parents are
too loving

In many adoptive families, parents are even more attentive and devoted to their kids than in non-adoptive families. As an adopted teenager, you may find your parents more tolerant, more open to discussion, and more available to listen to your concerns. "I talk to my mom about everything," says Anne, age fourteen. "She's like a close friend. She understands me, gives me advice, and consoles me in a way that my friends don't get from their parents."

Some adoptive parents take their roles as parents even more seriously than non-adoptive parents. After all, they waited a long time for you, and had to go through a lot to make your adoption happen. Their bookshelves are filled with books about adoption. They talk with other adoptive parents to trade experiences. Many times, they're more open to discussion and more eager to create a positive relationship with you.

Some adopted teenagers feel even closer to their families than non-adopted kids, and they're proud of it. Your adoptive parents had to fight hard for the right to take care of you! This can be reassuring and comforting. "Adopted kids aren't accidents like some biological children," says Felicia. "Our parents really *really* wanted us."

But sometimes, this attachment can be overbearing. As a teenager, you're wanting more independence and freedom. You might think that your parents are too protective, and you blame it on the fact that you're adopted. You don't want to be treated differently from your friends.

Some psychologists say things like, "Adoptive parents are often overprotective toward their children." Or, "Adoptive parents really feel that they must succeed at parenting, or else they're a huge failure. They do not realize that in being like this they risk stifling their child." In other words, sometimes adoptive parents, by being *too* loving, by doting too much on their kids, prevent them from blossoming into independent young people. They're so focused on keeping their adopted kids from having a rough time that they forget that the rough times are part of growing up.

How annoying—especially when you're all about getting out of the house and hanging with your friends! But don't forget . . . you're not the only one in the world with overprotective parents. There's no question that many of your friends are facing the same situation.

Being adopted, along with those lingering fears of abandonment, makes for a complicated relationship with your parents. And for some adopted kids, this means staying as close as possible to their parents and not busting out on their own and standing as individuals. These teenagers find staying in the shadows easier.

Other adopted teenagers live in a different way. They become very distant toward their parents, keeping secrets about how they spend their time. They aren't secretive because they're misbehaving, they just prefer to keep a sense of independence about their lives. It's as if they're building a world for themselves in which they don't need their parents . . . just in case they're "abandoned" again.

Confused yet? Well, think of it this way. The important thing to know is that a lot of these feelings you might be having (even feelings we don't cover in this book), are totally normal. They don't mean you're completely crazy. They just mean that you're a teenager.

parents who try to make everything

all right

Some adoptive parents feel like they have to be Superparents! They think that because their adopted children started life in an unusual way they have to make up for it by overdoing the parenting. They push their children in school, they encourage sports, music, and activities. They're like soccer parents gone crazy!

Studies show there are a couple reasons for this. According to statistics, most adoptive parents are more educated, driven, and wealthy than most non-adoptive parents. They are more interested in making sure their children grow up to be intelligent, professional, and cultured—just like themselves.

Another reason, according to the experts, is that there's a deep feeling in many adoptive parents that they need to "heal" you. They assume that you were deprived of love in some way since you weren't able to be with your birth parents at the beginning of your life, and that they need to make up for this by overparenting.

Sometimes adoptive parents imagine what your future would have been like if they hadn't adopted you. Perhaps you would have been passed from foster family to foster family, or perhaps you would have been stuck in an orphanage in your country of birth. They feel like they want to "make up" for these possibilities by being really good parents.

But they also have certain feelings inside them that play out in their relationship with you. For one thing, many adoptive parents were unable to have children of their own, and they may feel some insecurity about this. But since they're able to raise amazing children (like you) they should be able to get over some of those feelings.

Parents can also go too far and be too demanding. One adopted teen, Eric, is convinced that he has a future as a football star and, in fact, he is the best player on his school team. But his parents, who are very intellectually-focused, don't encourage this side of his personality. Unfortunately, he has to play on the sly, and this causes stress on their relationship. Eric blames the situation on his adoption. But don't many non-adopted kids have to deal with the same issues of having different goals and dreams than their parents?

All parents, biological and adoptive, want the best for their children—because they love them.

If, like Eric, you find that your parents' expectations are a little too high, or that they don't pay attention to what you really want to do, it's important to keep the conversation going. You can't hide your dreams, and even if they don't agree with them, you have to do your best to talk to your parents openly about the disconnect.

your parents and your
background

Some adoptive parents tend to gloss over their children's backgrounds, focusing instead on their lives as they are now. But some adoptive parents make a much bigger deal about their adopted kid's origins. They tell the story of the adoption, over and over, in an attempt to have a completely honest relationship with their children.

Gone are the days of hiding an adoption. Very few adopted kids don't know the truth about their origins. After all, we as a society have learned how hurtful it can be to have family secrets like that. They always come out in the end—it's much better to be honest from the beginning.

Some adoptive parents won't shut up about it! They talk about adoption constantly. They celebrate two birthdays for you . . . your true birthday, as well as the day you came into their family. If you come from another country like Vietnam or Brazil, they'll try and make Vietnamese meals or play Brazilian music all the time. They do this because they want you to be proud of your origins or feel some connection to your culture, but it can make you feel like a freak, too. Everyone is different— some kids really like to affiliate themselves with their "roots," others don't. It's as simple as that, and the choice is yours.

Of course, all this comes from love, and because your parents want to do the right thing and respect your origins. They remind you about your past because they want to make sure that you understand your history, and that you're proud of it. They want you to be confident and clear about how important and unique you are. It doesn't mean they think you're a stranger, even if they go overboard. Feel free to tell them to take it down a notch. For example, Henry is a Korean teen adopted by a white family and he had to tell his parents to quit serving him *KimChee* or other Korean foods, which he doesn't even like, because he'd rather have burgers!

parents
who don't
do enough

Then there's the adoptive parents who seem like they're practically ignoring the fact that their kids were adopted. They tell you the story once or twice, then never mention it again. As far as they're concerned, your life began the day you came into their family. They don't talk much about where you came from or what your circumstances were. Sometimes it's because they don't know that much. Sometimes they just don't want to make you feel like you're different. Sometimes it's because they don't want to encourage painful memories, thinking you'll fit in better if you just ignore all that stuff.

But these parents can go too far, as well, and it's confusing, especially for kids who are from a different ethnic background than their parents. After all, there are lots of questions to be answered, and by not answering them, it's like devaluing how important they really are.

Remember that your adoption is a totally acceptable topic of conversation. Even if they don't want to discuss it, your desire to want answers is normal and healthy.

Some adoptive parents get confused in the parenting process. They see you struggling at school or having a hard time with your friends, and they blame these issues on your adoption, too. Or worse, they make

excuses for you based on the fact that you're from a different culture.
If you're not fitting in, they may think it's a problem of your past.
These scenarios can be very hurtful. After all, you have the same
potential as anyone else. Your response? To never, *ever* undervalue
yourself, no matter what attitude your parents have. It's your life.

the legacy
of adoption

All teens, adopted or not, have some clashes with their parents. It's important for you to establish your own identity, and usually this means defining yourself separately from your parents. For some of you, this means rebelling, or even misbehaving. But let's face it, non-adopted kids rebel all the time.

But some adopted teens have a deep sense of guilt or debt to their parents. You're constantly reminded by society how lucky you are to have found a loving home, and you feel that it's because of their kindness and love that your current life is even possible. They gave you a home, fed you, gave you love, and sent you to school. What would life have been like without them?

So rebelling, then, becomes more complicated. The last thing you want to hear when you get a mohawk or dye your eyebrows pink is "After all we've done for you!" It makes you feel ungrateful, disloyal—bad. It gives the whole process of rebellion an extra layer, and it's not easy.

It's really important, as an adopted teen, to keep in mind that the feelings of disloyalty or ungratefulness aren't all that different from other kids. They, too, get the whole "After all we've done for you!" speech.

And also, don't forget that you're not the only person who benefited from your adoption. Your parents got something out of it, too. They got *you*. You brought joy and meaning to their lives.

As an adopted teenager, it's all about experiencing your life as it comes, regardless of how and where you started out. You have to be yourself and stand apart from your parents, just like other teens. It's your job.

you are not my real parents

Some adopted teenagers use their adoption as an excuse to rebel even further. "You can't give me a curfew! You're not even my real mother!" or even "I didn't ask you to adopt me!" You can imagine how much these words hurt.

It is often Mom who gets the worst of it. Catherine, an adoptive mother, experiences this every day with her thirteen-year-old son, Tony. "He never questions his father," she says, "On the other hand, he sees me as a rival to his biological mother. We went through a very difficult time when he called me all sorts of names."

It is normal to feel anger toward your parents for a while during your teens, whether you're adopted or not, and it's healthy to express it. It doesn't mean that you don't love them, or that you reject them as parents. It just means you're a teenager, and that you've actually

accepted them as your parents. (Otherwise, why would you bother rebelling against them?)

Your parents, hopefully, will recognize this as a positive development. You're a teenager, and like any normal teen, you're rebelling against your parents. It means you're right on track and going through all of the normal stages of growing up.

Some psychiatrists would say that this anger is actually aimed at your birth parents, whether you know them or not, from a deep-seeded frustration at having been "abandoned." (Great, you're thinking, *that* word again.) Anyway, because your birth parents aren't around, sometimes you lash out at your adoptive parents instead. They're much easier targets.

This may or may not be true, and certainly isn't true for everyone, but considering it might help you sort out your own feelings. In any case, as tough as it may be to deal with some of your frustrations, try to keep in the back of your mind how important your parents are in your life.

teens like any
others

No matter what kind of crisis is going on in your life these days, remember that it's probably not because of your adoption. Remind yourself that every teenager feels like their parents don't understand them. Just because you're adopted doesn't mean that you're any more or less of a stranger to your family. Everyone has drama during their teens, adopted or not.

It's important to express yourself to your parents but, let's be honest, sometimes you totally overdo it. You say things you don't really mean ("I hate you!") and throw stuff. You may become depressed, run away, even experiment with drinking, or drugs. You might reject your family in a really self-destructive way.

Some psychiatrists say this is all about putting your parents' love to the test, like you're making sure they really care about you in spite of your totally ill behavior. And guess what—they will always love you. (But that doesn't mean you should make them miserable just because you can.)

It might make it easier on you and your parents if you try to explain some of the things you're feeling. And remember, it's always worth it to get help from someone else—a teacher, a school counselor, even a good friend. No matter how bad things are, it can't hurt to talk it out a little.

parental
worries

Don't forget, your parents are people, too, and any crisis you're going through is also a crisis for them. They are trying to be understanding and, let's be honest, it can't be easy trying to guess what freak-out you'll have next time! They're also being reminded that, no matter what the situation has been up until now, one day you're going to grow up and move away from them.

Adoptive parents especially have it tough during this time. They went through a lot to gain the right to raise you, and hearing things like "You're not my real mother!" can really hurt—badly.

Adoptive parents also freak out about whether or not they've failed as parents. They start wondering if they're to blame for your frustrations or if you're rejecting them because they did a bad job.

Some adoptive parents cave in at this point, which is unfortunate. It's important for them, and for you, to respect their roles. Like it or not, they're your parents, and that's that. They have the right, and the duty, to set rules and enforce them, whether they're your biological parents or not.

relationships with

brothers
and sisters

Relationships between adopted brothers and sisters aren't usually that different than those between biological brothers and sisters. You play together, fight together, eat together, and live together. You have bonds and rivalries. There may be one sibling you really like, and another one you can't stand. But you all share an understanding about your family and your parents that no one else will ever know.

You probably don't talk about your adoption all that much with your siblings. If you and your siblings were adopted later, you might discuss life before your adoption, but you might not.

However, the arrival of a new, adopted child in the family can make older siblings jealous, especially older non-adopted children. Kind of like how a new baby can annoy the stuffing out of an older sister!

This happens in every family. But when the jealousy involves an adopted sibling, it's scary because it opens up the fear that perhaps you don't fit into this family after all. You might worry that your parents love their other children more than they love you.

It's important to realize that it's not like your parents only have a certain amount of love. It's not going to run out, no matter how many siblings there are. And besides, you're lucky to have siblings to play with, fight with, and share with. You'll need them later on in life.

the extended
family

As if it's not challenging enough to deal with your parents and your siblings, you've also got a whole extended family to figure out. Grandparents, uncles, aunts, cousins . . . you name it, they're there, and they play a very important role in your adoption. Usually, they're just as psyched as everyone else about your adoption, and they view you as an important part of the family. They also know how hard your parents had to work to get the right to raise you, and they appreciate the love you've brought into their house.

But sometimes, you'll come across a family member, perhaps a grandparent or aunt, who doesn't understand what adoption is all about, and who treats you differently from the family's biological children. They aren't unkind or neglectful, but they find ways to point out your differences, and this can hurt.

Most grandparents, even the ones who don't understand everything right up front, end up forming special and affectionate relationships with adopted grandkids. One adopted teenager who we met earlier, Tatiana, had such a special relationship with her grandmother that before she died, her grandmother left her the necklace she hadn't taken off for decades.

You're lucky to have these people in your life. They give you per-
spective and understanding about the world and your family. Their
stories and lessons will stay with you forever.

But some grandparents come from a different time, when adoption
wasn't as common or as celebrated as it is these days. They get weird
about things, and it can be really annoying. For example, one day Nick
and Amy's grandmother said, "Get out of the kitchen! I'm baking cook-

ies with my grandchildren!" She was talking about her two "biological" grandchildren, Nick and Amy's cousins, and it hurt. When Nick and Amy told their mother about it, she was furious. She stood up to their grandmother, and it helped make Nick and Amy feel much better. They knew they were as much a part of the family as the others.

I really want to know

WHERE DID

You're

still

A chip off the
old block

I don't need
to know

COME FROM?

you.

i don't
need to
know

Most teenagers don't have much interest in their backgrounds. There are too many other things to think about. School. Friends. Sports. And the big one—puberty. Your favorite topic.

Let's face it, finding out about your roots can wait until you figure out where that hair is coming from.

Many adopted kids feel the same way. They've found a home, they're in their families. Why do they need to know any more? Besides, knowing all that information can open up all sorts of insecurities about whether they belong or fit in. They wonder how or why an understanding about their birth parents and origins should make any difference. "I'm not part of their lives, and they're not part of mine," says Alice. "I respect them, but I don't love them. I don't even know them!"

Not everyone understands these feelings, and you may feel pressure from friends or family to find out the truth about your birth parents. They assume you'd want to know your history. But if you don't, you don't, and it's no one's business but your own.

It can get even more annoying when you turn on the TV. Everywhere you look there's another segment or show about birth parents being reunited with their kids. But just because they show it on TV doesn't mean that's the way you have to go about things. Your decision to seek out your birth parents is your decision alone and you don't have to justify it to anyone. Enough said.

i really want to
know

Beyond the question of finding out about your birth parents, there's the question of finding out about your birth country. If you have a Chinese background, for example, or Russian, you might be interested in learning about that culture, or that language, or even that

My birth country is just as cool as home!

cuisine. Alex, who was born in Russia (remember him?), has been study-ing the Russian language. Nick, who was adopted in Morocco, loves to cook with his *tagine*. Learning these things can help you identify your own unique and special qualities, and your way of giving props to your roots.

Maybe you dream of going to your country of origin one day to get to know it better. Some of you might have already even made the trip. Nick's been back to Morocco twice, where he found the people friendly, kind, and eager to get to know him. He plans to learn Arabic one day.

This kind of trip isn't for everyone, but if you're feeling curious, and if your parents can afford it, it might be worth talking it over with them. After all, you represent more than one culture, superstar!

Some adopted kids from other countries even like to go so far as to visit the orphanage where they stayed, or make contact with the nurse who looked after them. They like to check out the town where they're from, eat the local food, and see the local sunset.

a chip off the
old block?

"I would just like to have a photo of my mom, so I know who I look like," said Tamara. She, like many adopted kids, doesn't have anyone at home to measure herself against. Will her nose flatten out, or sharpen up? Will she be taller than her new family, or shorter?

Not that it really matters, but it would be nice to know.

Also, for Tamara, a photo of her mother, or her parents, puts a face to the concept of a "birth mother," proving that she did, in fact, come from a real person, and not from outer space. (Even though many non-adopted kids believe that their parents are aliens, too.)

One common thing among adopted kids is a concern, or fear, that they've passed their birth mother on the street, or in the subway, and didn't even know it. Unconsciously, they scan faces in the street to see if they recognize themselves in the eyes and noses that walk by.

"What if that was her?" you ask. You wonder if you might meet them someday without realizing it. And having a photo would help put this idea to rest.

Think about it and talk it over with your parents. If you decide it's something you want to pursue, you might be able to find a photo through your adoption agency.

i don't want to hurt my adoptive
parents

Some adopted kids would love to know more about their
birth families, or travel to their country of origin, or have a photo of
their parents, but they're afraid to ask because they don't want to hurt
their adoptive parents.

If that's you, you might fear that your adoptive parents will think
you're unhappy with them or that you wish you'd stayed with your birth

family. You're worried they'll think you want to leave and go back with your birth parents. Crazy, right? Because this isn't what you're thinking at all!

You also might feel a bit guilty because you think that by saying you want to know about your birth family you're somehow "choosing" them over your parents. You don't want them to think you're ungrateful or that you're betraying them by wanting to know the truth. You're not being disloyal by seeking out the rest of the story.

But your parents are smarter than you think they are (trust us, it's true), and it's pretty likely that they understand your feelings or have realized that one day these questions would arise. Knowing your history is a basic right you have, and if you think about it, asking them for their help and support in a situation like this is exactly the kind of thing a child asks a parent.

Start by asking them about their role in your adoption. How did it come about? Why did they choose to do it? How did they find you? What do they know about where you came from, and who your birth mother is? What did they expect, and what did they find?

Many adoptive parents are eager to help their children. After all, remember that adoption works both ways . . . they've given you love and a home, but you've brought them many years of happiness.

i'm afraid of being
disappointed

Some adopted kids, deep down, are really afraid of being disappointed or unhappy with their birth parents. For years, you may have fantasized about who they are, imagining the worst-case scenarios (my mom was a criminal!) as well as the best (my mom's really a movie star!).

This isn't something that only adopted kids do. All children fantasize about what other circumstances they'd rather be in. They all invent new families for themselves. The only difference is that, as an adopted child, you have more fuel for the fire!

So when you're considering making the effort to find out the story of your birth mother, you start to wonder . . . what if it's a nightmare? What if your birth mother wants nothing to do with you? What if she's in prison? Or maybe worse, what if she is fabulously rich and happy? Or what if she's just a normal woman, with a normal family?

It's a lot to think about, maybe too much. But if you decide you want to find out the truth, let your adoptive family know. They're there for you.

Reuniting with your birth mother, if it happens, may be a very emotional experience. But it also may be a total letdown. After all, you've been thinking about her for so many years, it's impossible to guess how you'll feel when you meet her. Most adopted children who find their birth mother actually never see her a second time. They realize that their lives are so different now, and that their paths are so separate, that they have very little in common. But knowing they've completed the search, and put a face to the name, helps them close the chapter of wondering about the truth and get on with the business of living.

Of course, this isn't for everyone. Your life story can't be captured in a book, and we certainly can't predict what path you'll take. You'll write your own life story.

maybe some
other time . . .

Some adopted kids decide that they're entirely uninterested in finding out about their birth families. They've found a balance within their own family, and they're happy with their adoptive parents. They're looking forward to the future. So why rock the boat?

Don't think you're a freak if you're feeling this way. There is no rush to find out the story of your adoption, and only you can decide when or where or how to proceed—if at all. Many kids never go for it, and that's fine. But that doesn't mean you can't talk it over with your parents and seek out their support in making your decision. Remember, no matter what you decide, your adoptive parents love you, forever!

my
roots

For some adopted kids, there's no question. You have a strong desire to know what the deal is: where you came from, who your natural parents are, and what the story of your life is. You've overcome any feelings of guilt or doubt about how your adoptive family will deal, and you've decided you're going to pursue it, no matter what. Who are your parents? What do they do? Do they have other children? Are they alive?

Your questions are strong, and you've decided you need answers. It's not that you're lacking for emotional support but you want to know about your background, and knowing about your gene pool is definitely part of that. You carry your birth parents' genes, not your adopted family's, and you've decided you want this piece of the puzzle filled in once and for all.

Mostly, you're curious about your mother. Maybe you wonder if she was single when she gave you up? Maybe she had no choice? Maybe she was abandoned, too (by her family, or her husband, or by society)? In some countries, single, pregnant women have no other choice than to give their children away. Whatever the case, it's probably your mother who you're most interested in finding.

UNDERSTANDING

The biggest reason for wanting to know the truth and for undertaking this search is to answer the simple question: "Why?"

Maybe it was because your mother couldn't provide for you? Maybe your mother was from a country that was at war? Maybe she was too young for the responsibility? Maybe her family refused to accept a baby born outside marriage? Who knows?

One thing you must understand, and perhaps the search will help reinforce, is that it wasn't your fault. You were not thrown away.

Adoptions only happen in situations where it's impossible for the mother to take care of the baby. Almost all adoptions are better for the baby in the long run, and learning your story will likely confirm this. You'll have the confidence you need to move forward in life.

So, should you know the truth, even if it is disappointing? Maybe not now, but someday. Knowing the truth helps you to understand yourself. But understanding yourself is a lifelong adventure for everyone, not just adopted kids.

FOR MY HEALTH

There are also some practical reasons why you might want to know more about your origins. For one, there's your health. When doctors treat you, it helps for them to know about your "family medical history," that is, what physical strengths or weaknesses were passed to you by your biological parents. But adopted kids don't always know their family medical history. Some of them don't have the records they need, and learning about their birth families might help to clear things up.

The genes your birth parents gave you, besides making you tall or short, blonde or dark-haired, also determine some things about your health. For example, children with a parent who has diabetes may want to know about it so they can do what it takes to prevent it. Same for cancer, depression, and other health conditions. Knowing your birth parents' medical history can come in handy! Check with your adoption agency to see what you can find out.

who knows about my
background?

There are all kinds of reasons to find out the story of your birth parents, but it might not always be an easy task. Some adopted kids spend years trying to track down their birth mothers, only to find it's a dead end. Every state is different, and every country is different, and although many adoption agencies keep all the information you'll need right at hand, many don't.

Most likely, there's a file about you at the adoption agency that your parents used to find you. Depending on the agency, and when and where you were adopted, there might be information in that file about your birth parents and their lives. This information may be helpful to you emotionally, practically, or even medically, and it may answer all kinds of questions you have about who you are and where you came from.

But the file might also be a disappointment—just a birth date, an adoption date, and some information about the first few weeks of your life. One adopted teenager, Sandy, spent years working with her family to uncover her files, only to find that barely any information existed. Her file told her that her mother was brunette and took vitamin C. But that was it! There was no information about her ethnic background, where she was from, or where she lives now.

Finding information about your birth parents takes patience, bravery, and time. There's always the possibility that you won't find out anything, or perhaps worse—you'll find out things you didn't want to know. But many adopted kids find it necessary to learn what they can. If you're one of these adoptees, you'll have to work very closely with your adoptive parents to uncover the details.

taking one step
further

If your search for information makes you frustrated, it may make sense to turn to one of the many groups that help reunite birth parents with the children they gave up for adoption. Some of these groups are fabulous, and some are just out to make money, so it's important that you work with your adoptive parents and take your time. And remember: Whether you decide to find your birth parents or not, your life is just as full and rich as anyone else's. Even though your birth parents are an important part of your past, they are your past, and you've got a great future ahead, no matter what!

you're still

you

The truth is, most adopted kids never do find their birth parents, but they go on to have exciting, interesting lives. Sure, there's a frustration in never having complete closure on the questions they have, but when all is said and done, they're able to build happy, good futures. They get married, have kids of their own, and continue to be an important part of their adoptive families. Even though you don't have all the answers, it doesn't change the wonderful person you are.

doing some research

There are several Web sites devoted to adoptions and adopting, and they are a good place for you to start when you're looking for more information. Try these sites:

http://www.adopting.org

http://www.adoptionnetwork.com

http://www.adoption.com

suggestions for further reading

Where Are My Birth Parents?
by Karen Gravelle
(Walker Books for Young Readers, 1993)

Born in Our Hearts: Stories of Adoption
by Filis Casey and Marisa Catalina Casey
(HCI, 2004)

Twenty Things Adopted Kids Wish Their Adoptive Parents Knew
by Sherrie Eldridge
(Delta, 1999)

The Essential Adoption Handbook
by Colleen Alexander Roberts
(Taylor Trade Publishing, 1993)

The Adoption Resource Book
by Lois Gilman
(HarperResource, 1998)

Open Adoption Experience: Complete Guide for Adoptive and Birth Families—from Making the Decision Through the Child's Growing Years
by Louis Ruskai Melina
(Perennial Currents, 1993)

The Post-Adoption Blues: Overcoming the Unforeseen Challenges of Adoption
by Karen J. Foli and John R. Thompson
(Rodale Books, 2004)

Adoption Wisdom: A Guide to the Issues and Feelings of Adoption
by Marlou Russell
(Broken Branch Production, 1996)

index

about the authors

Anne Lanchon is a journalist who specializes in education and literature for children. She has published other helpful books for young readers.

Monike Czarnecki is a children's illustrator who also creates sets for the theater.

Tucker Shaw is the author of numerous novels and self-help books for young adults.